FROM THE WORD GO

NICK DRAKE

FROM THE WORD
GO

BLOODAXE BOOKS

ISBN: 978 1 85224 714 0

First published 2007 by
Bloodaxe Books Ltd,
Highgreen,
Tarset,
Northumberland NE48 1RP.

www.bloodaxebooks.com
For further information about Bloodaxe titles
please visit our website or write to
the above address for a catalogue.

Bloodaxe Books Ltd acknowledges
the financial assistance of
Arts Council England, North East.

Cover design: Neil Astley & Pamela Robertson-Pearce.

Cover printing: J. Thomson Colour Printers Ltd, Glasgow.

Printed in Great Britain by
Bell & Bain Limited, Glasgow, Scotland.

'And with one bound he was free...'
(UNKNOWN)

ACKNOWLEDGEMENTS

'Live Air' was first published by the *Independent on Sunday*.

I am deeply indebted to Dave Stagg for his detailed commentary and suggestions on the poems in *Boxes*.

Thanks to John Mole and Jackie Kay for reading and responding so helpfully.

I'd also like to thank the Civitella Ranieri Foundation for a Fellowship in 2005; and the Poetry Book Society for their Next Generation promotion.

Thanks also to Paul Rainbow, Greg Dean, Brenda Manning, Simon Coury, Chris Cherry and Jeremy Goldney.

CONTENTS

I

BOXES

Mangoes

I got the mangoes cheap in the Arndale arcade;
Appraising them, he pressed a yellow thumb
Into the flesh, like the haematologist who worked
His watery legs; they held the impression
For a minute. Not good. I'd hoped a mango might
Summon its fabulous country of origin,
Its women and waters, heat and orange sunsets –
On a knife he showed me a slice, still green;
'See? Unripe, and never like the real thing
If ever you've tasted them fresh from the tree.'
So his last supper was chocolate milk and pills;
He insisted I throw the fruit away;
I arranged them on a plate, indigestible
Sweet still life, composed, decomposing.

His Model Railway

First he'd heat the carving-knife steel blue
In the gas flame, sweating in the kitchen
To perform his miracles on polystyrene;
Slicing the light atoms before they fused
Into mountainsides and pastoral domains,
Painted and forested by their careful god;
And a model village, uninhabited;
Police station, town hall, railway station;

The 0-guage-track returning perpetually
A train powered by mysterious pyrites
Before the time of timetables and snows;
We watched from the borderlands of shadow,
The hushed enthusiasts of his creation
Under the attic light-bulb's fragile moon.

Books

How did he find the book in my anorak pocket?

He sat me down at the kitchen table, face
To angry face across the white formica;
Like chess-pieces the salt and pepper shakers
Stood for black and white, for truth and lies.

'Look at me. Who gave you this? Your teacher?
Do you not understand how millions,
Doctors and students, people like us, died
In ditches, skin and bone, because of *this*?'

I stared out of the window, nudged the pepper
Around the table, and maintained my silence.

He threw Mao's little red book in the rubbish bin.
'Words are dangerous. I know. I've *seen*...'

From then it was books of poems in my pocket.

Noir

He walked by night, the disillusioned gangster
Depending on darkness for his shadow power,
Fearing no evil, stylish, demanding truth,
Evading the reveal of dawn's weak light –

Or so I've got him down in my dark book;
An image made of paper and black ink;

Oppose this with a summer memory;
Driving through country lanes, all windows down,
A bag of plums between us; spitting stones
From his cool smile – how they shot away
Like bullets at his adversary, the wind
Which couldn't catch us; I fed him blue plums
As he drove into the harvest smoke's dead end –

Then out the other side, into the sun.

A New White Citroën DS

The apogee of executive success;
A new white Citroën DS, my father's
Dream car for the space age, futuristic
Headlights that swivelled like a robot shark
As he zoomed past the Escorts, Capris, Datsuns...
And his pride, the unique hydraulic suspension
That raised us as by antigravity
Eight inches closer to heaven. When he lost his job

It was surrendered, and he sat like Job
On his heap of nothings, circling vacancies;
And then his wife: mastering his cries
He climbed the stairs to his boys, a bag of clothes
And her warm rings in his fists, the burning eyes
And white face of the man who fell to Earth.

Time Machine

Appearing in his car on Sunday mornings
Impatient for the whole world to wake up,
He'd arrive for lunch before breakfast
And leave before his coffee could turn cold
Because it was *'a very long way back'* –
In one brief day, he'd find his savings shrunk,
The TV turned up high but no one home,
And his true love turned to ashes in a box.

He'd wait outside his own house in the dark,
In the driving seat with the dials' fantasy,
Dressed in his slippers, indigo pyjamas
And ancient sheepskin coat; insomniac
Watching the frost crawl the windscreen glass;
Then scrape it off in the strange light of Monday.

Monochromes

Net curtains of rain run slowly down to ice;
The streetlights trigger on at 4 P.M.;
The room's lit from low-angle, monochrome;
Along the shelves the family photographs
Like cut-out paper chains of shadow time;
A serious baby; a smart young officer;
A frizzy-haired student; a man with a long stare
And matinee idol hair; in this freeze-frame

Side by side we watch his favourite film;
Old soldier, silent son, holding hands;
Shadows escape down stairwell spirals;
The zither sounds; caught out, for the last time
Before he vanishes to the underworld,
A fall of light reveals the Third Man's smile.

Africa

He was puzzled by his dying; shook his head
At the prescriptions' great arcana
Translating white boxes and foil packets
Into gifts for the tongue;

                  he took his medicine,
Relishing the attentions of the nurses;
When they served his dinner or his pills
He'd flirt in Afrikaans to have them smile,
And name his favourite cities as their homes:
Nairobi, Kampala, Cape Town, Dar es Salaam...

When he had his 'accidents' he'd almost laugh,
Refuse the shame, and joke as we hosed him down
On hands and knees in a white hospital bath;
His mottled hide, his fleshless bones, his bellow:

An elephant in the graveyard of the zoo.

Lost in Space

Our last words spoken on the phone, across
The strains of distance, perhaps as if he knew
He'd die in the next hour; his voice was odd,
Lost in space; *'Are you ok...?' 'Ok...'*
I saw him settled in a delicate craft
Adjusting the gold receivers and blinking dials
Preparing for the one-way voyage to the stars;
It was his dream. Not sitting in a room
In a Brighton hospice counting down the seconds
In a high-backed chair, his plastic padded throne.
We said we loved each other; then fainter,
Light years further with each word's delay:
Goodbye, goodbye, goodbye, goodbye, goodbye...
Eventually I put the phone down first.

The Messenger

We turned and looked but he had disappeared;
No blue bolt of light – the sky was clear;
No tsunami rose from the green sea
With its haul of wrecks and gulls to stand over Brighton
And blow its houses down; the waves concurred
Their little roars, and no such things occurred.
And if he spoke – *And so this is the end*
Of all that I was, and the end of your long task
Of caring for me – for example, no one heard.
Perhaps a guiding spirit took his hand
As he slept, and gently introduced him
To himself without the pain of all his wrongs.
He disappeared beneath the planes' white trails,
And near the calling of the brightening shore.

Cast

I stare down at his face; he'd smiled at me
Three days before as he lay in his last bed
Alive with complaint and courage. Then I kissed him
Goodbye. Now this head propped on a cushion's
A plaster cast, frosty scarecrow stubble,
Stitched-shut eyes and January lips a crime
Reconstruction from another century –
In the morgue toilet's fluorescent silence,
I bend over a white porcelain basin;
The twin taps of forgiveness and despair;
I mix them, cup the hard south England water,
Calcined, in my hands, and wash my face;
Glance up; shadowed, framed, caught by the mirror;
His grey hair on my head; his old grey stare.

Cartographer

Along the study wall, maps of his world
Representing history's shades and borders
Of Empires and countries he still recognised;
With colour-coded drawing-pins he tracked
Like a cryptic autobiography
Every place he'd visited or stayed –
Hundreds of pinheads, capitals and nowheres,
Down to this small room's last period.

Now he's dead, I unpin everything;
Hundreds of pinholes, like a tailor's pinking;
If only I could stitch an illuminated suit
From these charts' projections, legends and journeys,
To dress him properly for his last odyssey;
With a true and starry compass for his heart.

The Book of the Dead

Pastime for the soul on its night flight;

A bumper treasury of spells and prayers
To charm the demons of his worst nightmares?

His Negative Confession, true of heart?

Guide to the shadows of the catacombs
And the one path to the staircase of sunlight
And a world perfected like a summer suburb
Of peaceful fields, still parks and new estates?

A slim volume slipped into his pocket?

He'd say, make mine a good *read*, not literature
But a 007 thriller, girls and guns, white-
Knuckle, chase-sequence, ticking-clock disaster
Saved when he confronts the psycho Death
And coolly answers back his shibboleth.

The Snow Globe

Shake the snow globe to a sudden tempest –
In no-man's-land headlights investigate
Ruined columns and sectors of gravestones,
Black avenues and yews; precipitate
Strangers, uncles and aunts, grown-up children
Crossing the asphalt, hair freaked white on white;
The tolling bell signals the polished hearse
With its officers and absurd disguise of flowers

To this cold check-point; like the mystery man
Who defected from his own funeral without a trace,
His secrets pass now in this sealed coffin
But what is the exchange? The double cross
Of the silence in which we wait, our only clues
The dissolving puzzles of this gentle snow...

Last Things

His economy let nothing be thrown away
But saved for the rainy days of the after-life;
When we unsealed the airless, oily tomb
Of the garage we found his silver Honda,
And shelves of tins, sweetcorn and sauerkraut,
Cellars of olive oil, red wine, cheap honey,
Twenty canisters of fly-spray, boxes of salt,
And little canopic jars of nails and herbs.

Soon the place was empty, his life possessions
Parted from their shadows of no dust;
We kept the photographs; the rest we cast
With his last disposable razor and winnowed soap,
On the thriftless pyres of the rubbish dump;
The prodigals of his inheritance.

The Wardrobe

He always wished I'd grow into his shoes:
Still two sizes too big, old polished leather,
A horn bowed in each one, his benefaction
Determined for me because unlike my own,
Scuffed and disappointing: *'Surely you can afford...?'*
Polyester and nylon shirts and slacks,
The miracle clothing of his future and my past;
Old man, new ghost, now for the last time
He haunts me in the scents of this inheritance;
I gather all his ties in my throttling hands,
Browns and beiges, the decades of his labours;
Sliding and slithering, they will not be charmed
Into the black bin-bag; this makes me grin,
But handle them as if they're poisonous.

Boxes

In the dark hinterland of his wardrobe, hidden
Under static-ghosted nylon sheets I found
Three small boxes wrapped like birthday presents
Named but never given (his parents
And my mother: *Anna, Jan, Patricia*);

On each his inky warning: DO NOT OPEN
Like a curse upon the man who'd wake the dead
From their tin tombs, their shrines of secrecy...

I weighed in my cold hands their last remains;
Extinct, gritty ash in dated urns;

And now I have the set, a gift of ghosts
What should I do but return them to some light;
Opened, scattered like a white bouquet
At the end of the story; and then walk away...

To His Dead Ear

When he heard he was dying, then he began to speak;
At first in sweetness, then screaming down the phone
'Shut up! Shut up! Shut up!' Then cheerfully
As he lay in bed, the Don Juan of the ward;
'You're very beautiful, where are you from?'
He'd always been there, asked about their daughters
Nodding at me, the still unmarried son;
'He is a poet.' *'Just the one book, Dad...'*
Knowing he would embarrass me, he'd state
'It's nothing to be ashamed of.' And I'd mumble
My apology for poetry, and he'd almost smile,
Who knew the truth of silence, and its powers.
Perhaps he was right. And now he cannot answer
Back I speak these poems to his dead ear.

Daedalus

To escape the labyrinth of retribution
He fashioned two pairs of wings from seagull feathers,
One small, one large; we rose up in the air;
Beneath us the Minotaur wept, alone
In his palace of patterns. We turned to face the sea –
A dish of pewter hammered by the sun
With the maker's marks of ships, and the turned horizon
Invisible where the blue mirrored the blue.

My shoulder-blades are wingless; I outgrew
The little pair; to prove the story true
Of our strange journey, he hung them on the wall
Above the fire to see them from his bed;
At last he seemed a bird, so light and frail;
I closed his wings around him for a shroud.

II

Mud

From the word go
We were skinning the cats
Who sang another one
Which was music to our ears;
Then we counted the chickens
Before they hatched
By walking on the speckled shells
Until we lost count:
They were empty anyway.
There was nothing we couldn't break
But we saw no evil, and besides,
We'd done it now;
So we led the horse to water
But only the stones
Were still and deep;
We met the lambs coming from slaughter
And turned them back again
Down the war path
With its raindrops of blood;
When we came to a bridge
We crossed, then blew it up
Without looking back;
The river ran away with itself
Like smoke without fire.
On the other side, on the other hand
We stoned the crows,
Who had the last laugh
When we came to the house
Which had once been our home;
It was quiet as the graves
We had dug for everything,
And in a mirror on the bedroom wall
We found what we'd lost
On the other side of our faces;
And we remembered our name was Mud;
So we laughed over the spilt,
Spoiled things till we cried
And black feathers gently knocked us down
In the leaden silence
At the end of the day.

Babylon

These nights the summer's slowly burning down;
Under the moon's arc-light, the acetylene
Showers of traffic and the Perseids,
The shadow city stacks itself like cards.

Closer than for sixty centuries
Mars blinks in the sky, a small red eye,
A countdown warning sign or the TV's
On-button for the late news despatches;

Apartment towers and gardens in Baghdad
Shiver and collapse like cigarette ash;
The river-bed, an ancient pavement, cracks;

Leaves fray in the dark, not gold and red
But khaki, petrified, from the fused trees.

A sparkler of static, and the screen goes blank.

Graceland

They occupy the shambles of the palace;
Gold taps in bathrooms built by Ulster plumbers;
Baroque pavilions for barbecues;
Marble ballrooms with shattered chandeliers;
Parterres, cracked pools and desiccated fountains –
The mansion of power in this big shot age
Defended by six men, all Syrian
(Two shot, three fled, one hid inside a fridge).

Now US soldiers share out cigarettes
In clean fatigues; guns and battle helmets
Rest on coffee tables; composed and classical
For Associated Press they josh and smile,
These guys from Memphis and Appallachia
Cheering in the Dictator's private shower.

Boy Not Weeping (@Reuters)

Saved from the overnight archaeology
Of the bombing raid
An armless statue

No   an armless boy
Blackened torso   white bandages
Ali Ismael Abbas (photograph @Reuters)

A staring boy   biting his lips and tongue
Whose arms of flesh
End in blood and ghosts

But when he opens his mouth again
Does he cry
Lamentations   accusations   revenge?

No   he asks:
Will my new arms work? Can I eat
And play with them?

Sea Change

Under the balanced ball of the white sun
He lay on his back, abandoned by the tide;
Small flippers shrugged to his corpulent belly,
The comedian telling his last joke, mouth ajar,
Yellow canines like the razor-clam castellation
Of a sandcastle's eroded keep; the sea's
Withdrawn now, stood down, bored after the storm's
Jaw-jaw of repetitious khaki waves
Leaving drifting suds, and this grey creature,
Not an Emperor from a Chinese Opera
Surrounded by the shells of his concubines,
More a dead soldier in his combat jacket
On a bier of detritus, webbed in wreathes
Of sea-grass, frayed rope, plastic junk and sand,
Rendered from sea-change to the Promised land;
A sandpiper makes urgent enquiries of the breeze
Like a war reporter, nervous, for the sea
Reminds him of the meaning of his story.

Smile

Looters running a race in the midday sun
With crates of milk-powder balanced on their heads

Chased by troops in shorts and baseball caps
Armed with SA-80s and camouflage nets

Corporal astride his grinning captive
Surfer-style
                    The laughing loser trussed
And hung from a forklift truck
                                        Nude
Prisoners alluring for their centrefold

Thumbs up she beams over birthday boy
Above the cling film his Halloween mask
Cracked up with her for the camera

Posed on a box   his arms spread wide   trick wires
Running from his fingers and (cropped) cock:

Keep very still   ready or not   and: *smile*.

The Empire of After

A minor apocalypse
Of heat triggered
This repossession; seeds
Blown into standing legions –
Bristling conscripts in camouflage
Patrol the welded streams
Of railway lines;
Giant hogweed
Listening stations
Tuned to the megahertz
Of the sun,
Its glorious leader;
Divining the ghost passages
Of old bicycle spokes,
the radioactive decay
Of siding clinker's
Millennia,
And the corrugated hum
From the cattle shed
At the end of the lane
Where the white lines
Cease
Dash dash dash dash dash
And then silence
At the unmanned border
Of the Empire of After

Mist

Winter trees –
A cuneiform
Whose last living speakers –
Its muezzin calls and war cries –
Are crows, patrolling
Their territory of stones and sticks,
Crossing the stuck
Sea of mud
In forays and sorties
To the disputed border;
Rich pickings,
Shreds of evidence,
Tins and papers,
Smeared features and feathers;
By a service station
In its defence of light
A giant plastic chicken
Idol with its head in the clouds
While the convoys
Of juggernauts and saloons
With small music and chatter
Pass, between stations, lost
In the mist.

The Cake

Was it in a film or in a dream –
Time's flickering polka, silent, monochrome;

Old women around a table in black scarves
Faces like abandoned balloons as if

Their only sons had died at the last stroke
Of the clasped hands of the clock of midnight luck;

Then a waiter in a black suit brought a cake
And divided it; they wept but brought their forks

Up to their mouths' wet purses, as the salt
Tears dripped from their chins into the sweet;

And like a broken promise now fulfilled
Or a long-lost flavour found, they had to smile –

But then their mouths were empty; they wept again –
And so it happened until all the cake was gone.

They stared at the plate's empty mystery,
Wiped their eyes, and went into the snows

That had gathered at the window while they ate
Like the icing on the cake; in the dark night

Staring from the last frame of the film
The waiter with my face in the empty room

Dreaming of the cake, its crowded candles bright;
Making his wish, then blowing them all out.

c/o the Sea at Patea
(in memory of Paul Winstanley)

I'd guess you thought of your life as a book
Of short stories, unpublished, their integrity
Ghosted by the rejection letters you kept
And replied to; or so I believe, who figured
In the months we coincided in the Alpujarras;
You in a derelict mill, in the one deckchair
Placed at the edge of a doorway into air
And evening light, the steps long gone, below
God's handful of scattered river rocks,
The river always awol but for the glints
Of currents in the silver of the stones;
In the distance, balanced terraces
Of oranges, olives, and white villages –
Almost, perhaps, an image of your ideal
Of a good life for all; food, land, dignity,
The kind of thing we'd drink to – I was young,
You were wiser – in the local wine
Rough as the tire-treads of our hippy sandals.
Then with your habitual economy
You packed yourself, your books, stones, recipes,
And hundreds of tapes into the old green tin
Of the favoured 2CV, and moved on again...
After a few letters we lost touch –
Until your memorial, and here you are
In photographs as everybody knew you;
Bald, bespectacled, moustached, that careful smile,
Like a comic we knew better than to name;
Lover of music, and bacon; detester of tissues;
And all the other stories I didn't know;
Pink Floyd roadie, potter, furniture maker,
Greenpeace engineer, political letter-writer;
'A life,' as you once wrote, 'seen as a whole –
As much as there was ever going to be.'
And finally here's the fisherman with his trophies
In the soft fawn cowboy hat now laid to rest
Beneath the cuttings of the local man
Who died, fishing, on New Year's Day. My dear,
(As you would say) I know it's far too late

To write a letter of any kind but this,
But I must, if only to stamp and post
With its best wishes and conditionals,
To Paul Winstanley c/o the Sea at Patea,
Your final and unchanging home address.

Grave Goods

Her sheepskin coat   purse in the pocket
Hong Kong dragon   on a silk jacket

Charm bracelet   locket heart
The faithful dog   Ship of Good Hope

A cupid bow   time's silver arrow
These twenty-five years   precisely tonight

71,725 days   1,721,400 hours
Too many to thread   to hold or tell

So what should I leave   as counters or measures –
Blue pebbles for years   green coins for days

And for the winter's   tale of eternity
A pair of slippers   my childish gift

Of suede and wool   like the Egyptian lady's
3000 years in the tomb   and still prêt-à-porter

The Age of Analogue

(for Peter Hobson)

The tape you made for me ten years ago
In the month you died, in the Age of Analogue;

Recording the small hours on your black piano
In your long-lost living-room's auditorium;

Time's big bang radiation, the hiss and hum
Long after 'Some Day My Prince Will Come'.

A Box of Snow

Ticker-tape for winter's motorcade
Falling on skyscrapers and penthouse gardens;
As we leave the late night screening, two by two,
The city's a snow-globe, infinite avenues
Resolved to the street lamps' galaxies; we stand
Mesmerised, hands held up, faces turned,
Children again, at midnight, wide awake,
To receive the cryptic quantum of each flake;
Let's fill a matchbox with this moment's snow,
And believe every intricate, vanishing trace
Ciphers these angels under the Gotham eves,
Thirty-storey idols in training shoes
Scrolled down apartment blocks, tiny windows,
Frames from the city's advent calendar;
And us, together; keep it in your pocket;
I dare you, love, never to open it.

This Love

I looked for somewhere to leave this love.
I offered it to strangers in the street
Who backed away casting curses and coins.
I wrestled it into a black bin-bag
And drove it out of town to the very dark
Highway and abandoned it where the cars
Hissed and blared; I thought it might
Lose itself on the wrong side of the forest,
Or end as road kill. But this hollow dawn
It was back, scratching at the window glass.
Will you feed its insatiable hunger
And stroke its wet head when it cries in its dreams;
Or will you send it away when it stares
Deep into your eyes, begging for its life?

A Glass of Water

I let you sleep to watch you sleeping;
Your hair's endearing loss of dignity;
The birthday present of your nakedness;
Perhaps I'll catch you laughing or shouting *Taxi!*;
I'd like to join you in your private dream,
And hold you in the vigil of my arms
In time-honoured fashion for a poem,
Guarded by our quartz clocks' set alarms.
But I see beyond closed eyes, warm skin, you
Briefly free of clocks, and love, and me;
And I drink to this from the bedside glass of water
Which has seen everything, is still and clear
Then empty in the dark; and so I'll sleep
And remember almost nothing when I wake up.

Rain Bird

Are you listening to the rain in our dream?
It is the many thousand languages
Whispered from ghost to ghost and time to time,
Our earthly messages: *can you hear me?*
Are you still there? How close can I hold you
So I no longer know where my skin ends
And yours begins? How can I let you go,
And how say goodbye? Then a night bird
Tunes up in his grove of shadows to the hushed
Tiers and gods of the city in the dark
And quiet rain; *'He sounds lonely'*... *'Shhh –*
It's a rain bird, he only sings when it rains: listen...'
So we do, and he does, and his music
Precipitates the first light, and he's gone.

44

Who said at 44 we are who we are?

I look in the mirror on my birthday;
The fluorescent ghosts of my father and mother, yes;
But worse, a kind of pixilated shift
Turning my elements – smile, grey hair, brown eyes –
To a chromosomatic familiar
Once removed. Perhaps it is the strip-light
Over the mirror, and its flickers of error.

I opened my mother's albums of her life
Before; smiling with boyfriends not my father
– the galleries of might have been fathers –
Between the tissue paper of lost time;
And I thought, *good for her.* This black and white was colour
And life, not elegy; she smiles for the camera

And, as it turns out, for me, almost as if
Asking, as an afterthought, *who are you?*

The Double Crown

(for Gavin Cornwall)

In the underground chamber the electric chairs
Are occupied by comedians in black capes
Rehearsing their sad acts before the mirrors;

A "three-two-one", my regular buzz-cut
Executing the demented frizz
Inherited from my mother, now neither black nor white,

Deleted from my guillotined talking head
To the checkerboard floor; I am a chess piece
Which Gavin checkmates with a new idea

On the conundrum of my double crown;
'At the moment of conception you were a twin –
But you murdered him, and now all that remains

Are these binary stars on the dark side of your head…'
He twirls his scissors; my reflection sticks
Like the cross-eyed fool in an opposing wind

On the far side of the mirror – my dead-ringer
Crowned in light-bulbs, his lightning wink, his blank,
His laugh like an emptying drain in Australia.

Live Air

Sex, adventures, places, writing – these are the ingredients of romance. Not for English men, though. From Lord Byron to Nick Drake, the great English Romantic has been an effete, narcissistic poseur, neutered by his own blankness.

THE INDEPENDENT.

Not what was expected, April 16, 2000

Reviewer: **A reader** from UK

I made the unfortunate mistake of thinking this was some newly found material from the 70's singer/songwriter Nick Drake. Needless to say I was dissapointed.

| rate-review | POST | 6 | 4 | tg/cm/rating-revi | tg/stores/detail/-/ |
| tg/stores/detail/-/ | 1852244887250(| | | | |

Was this review helpful to you? (YES) (NO)

AMAZON WEBSITE, READER REVIEW OF
The Man in the White Suit

The deserted second hand record exchange;
Just a bald guy and his ponytail
Guarding the memory palace of dead vinyl;
Multiple copies of *Rumours* and *Blue*
And the *Carpenters' Greatest Hits* in brown and gold;
Pink Moon's playing on the sound system,
Nick Drake's last LP; soon he would die
On the night Lord Lucan disappeared, Miss World
Lost her crown as an unmarried mother,
And the sun's November mercury slipped
Off the indigo horizon at 4.04 P.M...
I browse the bins, and luckily I find
Fruit Tree, the deleted posthumous box set –
Five Leaves Left, Bryter Layter, Pink Moon;
Three big black discs, acetate ammonites
Coded for ancient technology.
I offer Bela Lugosi my credit card;
He contemplates the name, my face, then up
To the shivering strip light and the obscure ceiling
Where sound waves collide with dust to conjure
Nick's sad ghost in the live air, whispering:
Know that I love you, know that I care,
Know that I see you, know I'm not there...
Then the song fades to recorded silence –
The hushed acoustic of his after-life –
Before the static, the perpetual heart-beat trip
Round the record's inevitable zero...

Lugosi stares from the dark vacancy,
The tangled wires, the drifting golden motes
In the creaky auditorium of dust
Where the ghost had sung and disappeared; he grins;
'Oh man, oh man, I thought you were *dead...*'

Zoroastrian

The prehistoric sun picks me out
On the blazing, high-noon black and white
Crossing of every deserted side street,
Fashionably dressed for once in light

Like the black summer zoot-suit
Of my attendant shadow, cut –
Detective, raven, zombie, tonto, saint –
From the superfine material of the moment.

The power of the glory of this heat;
No work, no history, no end in sight.
I take off my white t-shirt
And lie back on my silhouette

Orientated like a Zoroastrian
Praying for nothing to happen

Nick Drake was born in 1961, studied English at Cambridge, and then lived for several years in the Alpujarras mountains in southern Spain, where he helped to edit the *Letters of Robert Graves*. His pamphlet *Chocolate and Salt* (Mandeville Press, 1990) won an Eric Gregory Award (Society of Authors). His first book-length collection of poems, *The Man in the White Suit* (Bloodaxe Books, 1999), won the Forward Prize for Best First Collection. It was also a Poetry Book Society Recommendation and was selected for the Next Generation Poets promotion in 2004. His second collection, *From the Word Go*, was published by Bloodaxe in 2007. He has also published a critical study, *The Poetry of W.B. Yeats* (Penguin 1991).

Nick Drake's other books include *Nefertiti: The Book of the Dead* (Bantam/Transworld, 2006), the first of a trilogy of historical detective novels set over 30 revolutionary years in 18th Dynasty Egypt, and featuring the detective Rahotep. The second book will be published in Spring 2008. Rights to the trilogy have been sold to 14 different territories, including the USA, Spain, Italy, France and Russia.

He adapted the acclaimed memoir *Romulus My Father* (Text Publishing) by Raimond Gaita as a feature film for Arena Films (starring Eric Bana and Franka Potente) released in 2007. His stage adaptations include *To Reach the Clouds* by Philippe Petit (an account of his highwire walk between the Twin Towers in 1974) which Giles Croft directed at Nottingham Playhouse in 2006, and most recently, Anna Funder's prizewinning *Stasiland* for the National Theatre.

His first play, *Angel*, commissioned by The Shadow Factory, premièred at Salisbury Playhouse in 2002, was revived in Bristol Old Vic Studio's new writing season in 2003 and broadcast on BBC Radio 3 in 2005 under the title *Mr Sweet Talk*. He has also written several versions and translations of Spanish drama, including *Peribañez* by Lope de Vega, performed at the Cambridge Arts Theatre, and *The Burned Garden* by Juan Mayorga, performed at London's Royal Court in 1997.

He was Literary Manager at the Bush Theatre, London, from 1990 to 1994, and then Head of Development at Intermedia Films until 2002, working closely on the creative development of projects including the Oscar-nominated *Hilary and Jackie, Enigma, Iris, Sliding Doors* and *The Quiet American*.